THE HISTORY OF JUNETEENTH

BY MAXIMILIAN SMITH

Gareth Stevens
PUBLISHING

Library of Congress Cataloging-in-Publication Data

Smith, Maximilian.
 The history of Juneteenth / Maximilian Smith.
     pages cm. — (The history of our holidays)
 Includes bibliographical references and index.
 ISBN 978-1-4824-3894-9 (pbk.)
 ISBN 978-1-4824-3895-6 (6 pack)
 ISBN 978-1-4824-3896-3 (library binding)
 1. Juneteenth—Juvenile literature. 2. Slaves—Emancipation—Texas—Juvenile literature.
 3. African Americans—Texas—Galveston—History—Juvenile literature. 4. African Americans—Anniversaries, etc.—Juvenile literature. 5. African Americans—Social life and customs—Juvenile literature. 6. Slaves—Emancipation—United States—Juvenile literature. I. Title.
 E185.93.T4S55 2013
 394.263—dc23

                            2015018176

Published in 2016 by
Gareth Stevens Publishing
111 East 14th Street, Suite 349
New York, NY 10003

Copyright © 2016 Gareth Stevens Publishing

Designer: Sarah Liddell
Editor: Therese Shea

Photo credits: Cover, p. 1 John Leyba/Contributor/Denver Post/Getty Images; p. 5 Kathryn Scott Osler/Contributor/Getty Images; p. 7 Thuresson/Wikimedia Commons; p. 9 Hohum/Wikimedia Commons; p. 11 Everett Historical/Shutterstock.com; p. 13 Centpacrr/Wikimedia Commons; p. 15 Morgan Riley/Wikimedia Commons; p. 17 BotMultiChillT/Wikimedia Commons; p. 19 (top) Boston Globe/Contributor/Getty Images; p. 19 (bottom) Craig F. Walker/Contributor/Getty Images; p. 21 Joe Amon/Contributor/Getty Images.

Printed in the United States of America

CPSIA compliance information: Batch #CW16GS: For further information contact Gareth Stevens, New York, New York at 1-800-542-2595.

CONTENTS

Another Independence Day. 4

The Civil War 6

The Emancipation Proclamation . . 8

The First Celebration 12

Juneteenth Today. 16

Glossary 22

For More Information. 23

Index. 24

Boldface words appear in the glossary.

Another Independence Day

In the United States, **Independence** Day is July 4. However, there's another independence day **celebrated** on June 19. It honors the special day in 1865 when **slaves** in Texas were told they were free at last.

The Civil War

Slavery was one reason for the American Civil War, which was fought between 1861 and 1865. Many people wanted slavery to end, while others wanted it to continue. Some states left the **Union** and became the **Confederate States of America**.

The Emancipation Proclamation

On January 1, 1863, US president Abraham Lincoln **issued** the Emancipation Proclamation. Emancipation is the act of freeing. Lincoln's proclamation, or statement, freed more than 3 million slaves living in Confederate states.

9

Some of the freed slaves escaped and joined the Union army. However, many slaves never received the news. By the end of May 1865, all Confederate armies had surrendered, or given up. Yet, some slaves still didn't know they were free!

The First Celebration

On June 19, 1865, Union soldiers led by General Gordon Granger arrived in Galveston, Texas. This was more than 2 years after the Emancipation Proclamation. The soldiers told the slaves there that they had been freed. The slaves began to celebrate.

General
Gordon Granger

13

On June 19, 1866, a year later, former slaves in Texas again celebrated hearing the news. They prayed, sang special songs, and wore new clothes. Even after they moved away, many blacks returned to Galveston to celebrate June 19 each year.

Juneteenth Today

Today, June 19 is called
Juneteenth, Emancipation Day,
or Juneteenth Independence
Day. Many other states besides
Texas honor this day, and African
Americans aren't the only ones
celebrating. People of all races
take part.

17

Today's Juneteenth celebrations include prayer services and speeches in which African Americans remember and take pride in their past. There are also **rodeos** and **festivals** with special music, food, and dancing. Many towns and cities hold parades.

Even other countries celebrate Juneteenth! They set it aside as a special time to remember the end of slavery and the beginning of freedom. Next June 19, find a Juneteenth celebration near you—or start your own!

GLOSSARY

celebrate: to honor with special activities

Confederate States of America: the 11 Southern states that broke from the Union during the American Civil War

festival: a special time when something is celebrated

independence: freedom from control by another person or group of people

issue: to announce something in a public way

rodeo: a contest of many events involving cowboy skills

slave: one who is "owned" by another person and forced to work without pay

Union: the side of the Northern states in the American Civil War

FOR MORE INFORMATION

BOOKS

Murray, Julie. *Juneteenth*. Edina, MN: ABDO Publishing, 2012.

Otfinoski, Steven. *The Story of Juneteenth: An Interactive History Adventure*. North Mankato, MN: Capstone Press, 2015.

Peppas, Lynn. *Juneteenth*. New York, NY: Crabtree Publishing, 2011.

WEBSITES

History of Juneteenth
www.juneteenth.com/history.htm
Read more about this special holiday.

Juneteenth Links
www.socialstudiesforkids.com/subjects/juneteenth.htm
Check out the many Juneteenth links on this site.

INDEX

African Americans 16, 18

American Civil War 6

Confederate 6, 8, 10

Emancipation Day 16

Emancipation Proclamation 8, 12

festivals 18

Galveston 12, 14

Granger, Gordon 12

Juneteenth Independence Day 16

Lincoln, Abraham 8

parades 18

rodeos 18

slavery 6, 20

slaves 4, 8, 10, 12, 14

speeches 18

Texas 4, 12, 14, 16

Union 6, 10, 12